JOB INSECURITY
vs
LABOUR MARKET FLEXIBILITY

by David Smith

First published in February 1997
by
The Social Market Foundation
20, Queen Anne's Gate
London SW1H 9AA
Tel: 0171-222 7060 Fax: 0171-222 0310

Contributions to Policy No.2

ISBN 1 874097 61 5

Cover design by Adrian Taylor

Printed in Great Britain by
Xenogamy plc
Suite 2, Westcombe House
7-9 Stafford Road, Wallington, Surrey SM6 9AN
Typesetting by Wimyk Enterprises

CONTENTS

THE AUTHOR

DAVID SMITH is Economics Editor of the *Sunday Times* and was formerly Economics Correspondent of *The Times*. Before entering journalism, he worked for Lloyds Bank and the Henley Centre for Forecasting. His books include *The Rise and Fall of Monetarism*, *North and South*, *From Boom to Bust*, and *UK Current Economic Policy*. He is currently working on a book about the future of Europe.

ACKNOWLEDGEMENTS

Many thanks to Roderick Nye for suggesting this Paper at the very time I was most intrigued by the subject; also to many other people, but in particular to Peter Robinson of the Centre for Economic Performance at the London School of Economics and Professor Peter Spencer at Birkbeck College, for their useful perspectives. Evan Davis made helpful comments on the first draft. The usual disclaimers apply to any errors and omissions.

EDITOR'S NOTE

The following paper is the second in a series looking at the role of work experience in meeting the demands of a more flexible, modern labour market. The series marks the 25th anniversary of the Trident Trust, Britain's leading provider of work experience schemes for young people.

Foreword by John Spiers, Chairman of the Trident Trust

In this Paper, the second in a series of Trident Trust contributions to policy, commissioned and published in association with the Social Market Foundation, David Smith examines the relationship between job insecurity and Britain's move towards a more flexible labour market.

Popular belief has it that one is the inevitable price of the other. That as the labour market becomes more de-regulated and employers find it easier to hire and fire people, so workers become more vulnerable to the sack and jobs for life disappear.

Smith reveals a truer picture which is more complicated on both sides of the equation. Job tenure has declined, but only very slightly, over the last 20 years. Furthermore, the proportion of the workforce enjoying protection against unfair dismissal has actually risen over the last five years. Even the increase in part-time working is found to be overwhelmingly voluntary, while levels of temporary employment in Britain are much lower than in France, Germany, Sweden or Spain.

Nor, explains Smith, is the UK quite the model of an 'Anglo-Saxon' labour market that it is sometimes painted. Employment law reform has helped reduce structural unemployment in Britain, while that of our main European partners has risen. However, we have a long way to go before we can claim a labour market as aggressive and dynamic as America's, not least because our workforce is less geographically mobile.

General insecurity, then, has little basis in fact. However, its political resonance threatens to divert the attention of policymakers away from truly insecure groups such as the long-term unemployed.

Introduction

Harry Truman's famous remark in the 1950s, 'It's a recession when your neighbour loses his job; it's a depression when you lose yours,' has its modern-day parallel. Forty years on, and long after the abandonment of full employment as a formal policy goal by western governments, a new debate is raging in Britain. On one side, there is labour market flexibility, the breaking down of some of the old barriers and restrictive practices, which is seen to benefit the British economy. On the other, there is the apparent price of this flexibility — endemic job insecurity. One man's meat, in the form of flexibility, is, it appears, another's poison in the form of career uncertainty and the decline of permanent, full-time, salaried employment. The job for life has met its death. For every commentator, economist or politician praising Britain's new found flexibility, thousands of people are cursing, or are being encouraged to curse, the uncertainty and misery it has brought.

The purpose of this paper is not to deny the existence of all insecurity, it is to question whether it is as widespread as some have suggested. More importantly, it is also to challenge the idea that there is a trade-off between insecurity and flexibility. Insecurity, as I hope to demonstrate, is a loosely-defined concept which has many and varied roots. Genuine labour market flexibility, if it is a factor in creating temporary insecurity at all, plays a minor role. There is, in fact, a simple logic test that can be applied to the proposition that flexibility creates insecurity. It is by reference to the opposite proposition. Would anyone seriously argue that by making the market more inflexible there would be greater job security? Surely not. Blaming flexibility for insecurity falls into the same logical trap, the danger of which is that measures to enhance flexibility will be held up by the objections of the insecurity lobby.

This paper will also examine, critically, the claimed flexibility of Britain's labour market. There is a tendency to portray the reforms of the 1980s as being more far-reaching and fundamental than in fact they were, while forgetting that Britain's starting-point was that of a highly regulated and unionised labour market. The contrast with what came before may be a dramatic one. But while there have been many changes in some areas, notably trade union legislation, Britain's labour market has not suddenly decoupled itself from the rest of Europe. The notion of Britain as free market cuckoo in the European nest, conjured up by the European Commission and worn as a badge of pride by the government, suits both sides. Closer examination suggests, however, that this is a convenient, modern Euro-myth.

Chapter One: A Vogue for Insecurity

If one word has become the motif of the 1990s it is 'insecurity'. In truth 'insecurity' is a useful catch-all term. It at once invokes nostalgia for a lost world of stability and certainty, provides an explanation for changes in labour market behaviour, and offers a powerful explanation for discontent with the government. Insecurity is, according to those who trade in it, all-pervading, affecting those in low-paid jobs, well-paid jobs, and no jobs at all. It has become an essential tool for both politicians and journalists. A computer trawl through Britain's national newspapers in November 1996 found 2,778 stories dealing with insecurity over the most recent 12 months, 977 of them specifying job insecurity. A similar trawl, for the 12 month period from November 1985 to November 1996, a time when measured unemployment in Britain was some 50% higher at well over 3 million, showed just 234 stories on insecurity, and only 10 on job insecurity.

Insecurity, and the search for its cure, has been a theme taken up by many. The Commission on Social Justice, established by the late John Smith, set out, in its report, *Strategies for National Renewal*, what has become almost the received wisdom on the subject. 'For most people — those in the middle [of the income scale] — insecurity and anxiety are rife,' it said, adding, 'There is a definite disquiet and depression widespread in Britain. Many people who have the chance to work hard and to make themselves and their families better off are insecure about the future for themselves and their children, anxious about their jobs, scared about crime, worried about old age, and disillusioned with politics. Although nearly three times wealthier as a nation than we were in 1950, we are certainly not three times happier as a society.' (p.15)

The July 1995 report of the Commission on Wealth Creation and Social Cohesion, chaired by Lord Dahrendorf said, 'The decline of full-time tenured work, the emphasis on flexibility and competition, and the emergence of an excluded class is creating an insecure and fractured society with fewer and fewer shared values and common interests. Social cohesion is under stress.' (p.16)

Opinion polls have also detected this new age of anxiety, apparently built on insecurity. A Gallup poll for the *Daily Telegraph*, published in June 1996, showed that 76% of people believe their 'peace of mind' is worsening, against only 3% who thought it was improving. A generation ago, in 1968, when the question was asked, there was far less insecurity on this catch-all definition: 48% saw a worsening in 'peace of mind', and 14% an improvement. This is, of course, a broad definition of insecurity. Most people who invoke the word would claim that this broader insecurity has its roots in job insecurity. On the specific issue of job insecurity, an NOP poll for the *Sunday Times* in April 1996 asked people whether they worried that they or a member of their close family would lose their job over the next two years. In response, over half said they did indeed have such worries (23% were 'very worried', 28% 'fairly worried', making over half the sample, while 46% were not worried).

For the political parties, particularly those in opposition, insecurity is a gift. The more that people feel uncertain about jobs and careers, the less happy they feel with the incumbent government. Perceptions of insecurity, particularly among traditional Conservative supporters, are one reason for the disconnection between support for the Conservatives, as reflected in the opinion polls, and economic variables such as low mortgage rates and rising real incomes, which would normally be associated with a rising poll-rating for the government. For Labour, insecurity is a particular form of market failure. Insecurity neatly bridges the party's rediscovery of the virtues of markets, coupled with a desire to blunt some of their harsher consequences. Labour does not quite promise to eliminate insecurity, but it offers strong hints that this is a market failure that, in government, it would tackle. Thus Tony Blair: 'We live in a new age of anxiety ..... In this country over 1m people are on short-term or temporary contracts. Millions work part-time through necessity not choice. Youngsters who graduate can find work hard, even impossible, to come by. The gap between wages at the top and the bottom grows ever wider. A large part of today's workforce is burdened by insecurity, worried and undervalued, ambition blunted by fear. The days of a job for life are over.' (Speech to the Trades Union Congress, September 12 1995).

'The dominant feature of British economic life is widespread insecurity,' said Gordon Brown, the shadow chancellor, in September 1996. 'Thousands are experiencing downward mobility, millions live in fear of losing their jobs.' John Monks, general secretary of the Trades Union Congress, identified the market failure breeding insecurity in Britain as short-termism, and 'a financial system greedy for dividends'. Thus Monks, writing in The House Magazine, on November 4, 1996: 'The people who suffer most from this short-termism are the employees who lose their jobs. And we all have to live with the social and economic costs of unemployment. We are faced with a choice. It is, in a sense, a choice about what kind of capitalism we want to see. On the one hand there is an essentially Anglo-Saxon model based on hire and fire and short-termism. On the other there is a European model based on long-termism and social partnership: co-operation by all the stakeholders in an enterprise to promote their mutual interests.'

Monks's argument goes to the core of the debate about the nature of the shift towards a more flexible labour market in Britain and whether this, in combination with other special characteristics of the British economy, have provided a more fertile breeding-ground for insecurity than in other countries. Critics of the British approach would argue that, while globalisation has been a force affecting employment throughout the industrialised world, its effects have been exacerbated in Britain. Nor have only politicians, committees of the eminent and trade union leaders been the only ones to latch onto insecurity as the theme of the 1990s. The OECD, in its 1996 report on Britain, said: 'The market-based approach has yielded clear benefits in terms of job creation. But there has also been a marked widening in income inequality, some growth of temporary jobs, a perception of less job security, and a growing polarisation between work-rich and work-poor families.' (p.114) The Bank of England, in its May 1996 inflation report, wrote: 'The limited evidence suggests there has been a rise in job insecurity or in the perceived probability of unemployment among some groups of workers.' (p.36)

Britain's economic performance, although these bodies do not say so explicitly, is thus seen to be tarnished by the insecurity that has emerged as one of its by-products. The trade-off between growth and inflation has improved, the wage-price spiral is a thing of the past. Some of that, however, may be due to the fact that workers, fearful of losing their jobs, have been cowed into pay moderation. Critics are entitled to ask whether this is either healthy or tenable. But it is also appropriate to question whether this is an accurate description of Britain today.

Chapter Two: Defining Insecurity

Insecurity, 'a state of apprehensiveness of danger or loss', is by its nature almost impossible to pin down. If people tell opinion pollsters that they are insecure then assuming the polls are reliable representations of public opinion, there is insecurity. Ian Lang, the President of the Board of Trade, was criticised for saying, at the Confederation of British Industry's annual conference in November 1995, that job insecurity was 'a state of mind'. In fact, it is hard for insecurity to be anything other than a state of mind.

States of mind may reflect fashion or imitation, a kind of mild mass hysteria, but they are more likely to be based on events and experience. Suddenly, in the 1990s, everybody knew somebody, or knew somebody who knew somebody else, who one minute had been riding high, confidently climbing the career ladder, and the next was banking his or her redundancy cheque, with little prospect of finding an equivalent position elsewhere. When most commentators talk of insecurity, however, they appear to be combining, and often confusing, several different phenomena. Thus, insecurity is used to describe:

♦ A higher probability of unemployment, and greater involuntary job turnover, among those at the core of the labour market, people who could in the past rely, if not on a job for life, at least long-term stable employment. Thus, downsizing among large, previously paternalistic corporations such as the major clearing banks, or in the civil service, creates insecurity.

♦ The problems of those, not at the core, but at the periphery of the labour market. Thus, the relative decline in demand for unskilled workers, the problems of young people entering the labour market, the reluctance of employers to offer permanent jobs to new entrants, and the perceived bias against older people in employment are all elements of this insecurity. Will Hutton, in his stylised '30/30/40 society' has the middle 30% as 'marginalised and insecure': 'This is not the world of full-time jobs with employment protection and benefits such as pensions and paid holidays. Instead people in this category work at jobs that are insecure, poorly protected and carry few benefits ...... it includes the growing army of part-timers and casual workers.' (*The State We're In*, p.106)

♦ Those in long-term unemployment, including people forced to retire early because of lack of demand for their skills. Their problem may be locational or occupational, but it implies effective, and permanent, exclusion from the labour market.

Insecurity is sometimes, in addition, used to encompass income inequality, employment inequality (an 'unfair' distribution of jobs), or both. This is not the place to re-examine inequality. Suffice it to say that, while inequality may be a consequence of insecurity, the two are not synonymous. Insecurity should also, although it rarely is, be kept distinct from cyclical developments. Think, say, of the construction industry. Each time there is a recession in the industry, a certain number of people are laid off. But unless the lay-offs are becoming progressively larger, or more frequent, it would be wrong to conclude that this provides the basis for rising insecurity. In practice, things are a little more complicated than this. The 1990-92 recession had a relatively bigger impact on white-collar workers in southern England than its predecessor in 1980-81. This impact was still, however, a cyclical effect. It was widely interpreted by those on the receiving end, however, as the harbinger of prolonged uncertainty and insecurity.

Thus Matthew Symonds in *The Culture of Anxiety: the Middle Class in Crisis*: 'By and large, until 1990, recessions were something which other people bore the brunt of. Cosily insulated in the great corporate bureaucracies and their public sector counterparts, the world of lay-offs and redundancies was emotionally about as distant as the civil war in Bosnia. For middle-class professionals, once established in their chosen careers, exposed only to competition of the politest kind, the idea that a job for life might not be for life had yet to dawn. When such people talked about the need to 'shake things up', the importance of 'bracing change' or the unwisdom of attempting to 'buck the market', it was always others who stood in the way of economic progress and who would have to shape up or face the consequences. In short, nothing had prepared the middle classes for what was about to overtake them — a recession which would severely damage both their wealth and their job security.' (Social Market Foundation 1994, pp.9-10)

Clearly, it is possible to define insecurity in such a way that it takes in virtually every economic and social ill affecting the nation. That, however, would be both unmanageable and unhelpful. Clearly too, there is a danger of asymmetry about insecurity, in that those who become afflicted by it can make their discontent known, while those who acquire security become part of the silent majority. A common but imperfect measure of insecurity, for example, is average job tenure. In recent years there has been a small decline in tenure among men and a rather larger increase among women. One theory behind the 1990s vogue for insecurity is that it was driven by changes in working practices and the stability of employment affecting opinion-formers in the BBC, other media and the civil service. Thus, while far-reaching employment changes in manufacturing industry in the 1970s and 1980s were viewed by many as inevitable structural shifts in the economy, the 'white-collar' job shake-out of the 1990s was perceived, by those affected, as something altogether different, and much more sinister.

If we take the three possible components of insecurity — a higher probability of job loss at the core of the labour market, a greater number of people on its periphery and an increase in long-term unemployment — some objective evidence is available. That must be the first building-block in getting to grips with the question of whether, if people are indeed feeling more insecure, they are right to do so.

Chapter Three: Searching for Insecurity

The insecurity story is so much part of the current debate that the evidence for it might be expected to be much more clear-cut than it is. The statistical 'proof' of generalised job insecurity, in fact, barely exists. Part of this is because researchers are unsure of how best to measure it. Part of it is that it may be intrinsically unmeasurable. Mainly, I would argue, it is because the phenomenon has been exaggerated.

One of the most common measures of security is job tenure. According to the official Labour Force Survey, average job tenure for people in work has declined over the past 20 years, but only marginally. In the spring of 1975, the average job tenure of people then in work was 6 years, 1 month. By the spring of 1995 tenure has fallen to 5 years, 6 months. Within this, as noted earlier, tenure for men had dropped from an average of 8 years, 2 months to 6 years, 6 months, while tenure among women had increased from 4 years to 4 years, 7 months. Paul Gregg and Jonathan Wadsworth, writing in the Employment Policy Institute's Autumn 1996 Employment Audit suggest that tenure data may be biased upwards, because people, particularly those in the same job for long period, tend to exaggerate the length of time they have been employed. This may be true, but it should not affect the comparison with earlier data. Gregg and Wadsworth also imply that the fall in job tenure among men is a genuine reflection of labour market change, while women's increased tenure is probably due to greater use by them of maternity leave — they return to a job with the same employer after childbirth, rather than seeking a new employer. Even if this is also true, however, it is inconsistent with another frequent claim about insecurity in Britain — that it is due to employers, with the connivance of the government, exploiting an unregulated labour market.

The real point about job tenure is that it is a very poor measure of security. Rising tenure, paradoxically, can be associated with increasing insecurity, and vice versa. When the economy, and employment, are expanding, there are more opportunities for people to change jobs and, typically, average tenure will fall. Thus, overall job tenure reached a low of 4 years, 5 months in the Spring of 1990, at the end of the 1980s boom, since which time it has increased to its present 5 years, 6 months. The 1990s has thus been a period of rising tenure in comparison with the late 1980s. All this demonstrates is that there was a boom then but there has not been, so far, in the 1990s.

An unregulated, free-for-all labour market, with generalised insecurity, might also be expected to have huge swathes of the workforce without employment rights, and subject to the whims of their employers. Again, however, the evidence does not support that proposition. In 1975, employment rights, largely protection against unfair dismissal, extended to 94% of full-time workers and 77% of part-timers. At that time, employees gained such rights after six months in a full-time job, and after one-year as a part-timer. By 1985, after the Thatcher government had doubled, in each case, the period needed to acquire rights, the proportion of full-timers covered had dropped to 85% and, for part-timers, 58%. Five years later, following a further tightening of the qualification requirements for rights — to two years for full-timers and five years for part-time work — the proportions covered dropped to 70% and 30% respectively, and claims that Britain was well on the road to total labour market deregulation were rife.

Such conclusions were, however, premature. By 1995, as the economy and employment had recovered from recession, 74% of full-timers had employment rights and, following the successful test case which brought qualification periods for full- and part-timers into line — two years in each case- so did 57% of part-timers (broadly the same as the 1985 figure).

Surely, however, there is powerful evidence of insecurity in the rise of part-time and temporary work in Britain? The rise of part-time work is not a recent development. In 1951, 4% of total employment in Britain was in part-time jobs, rising to 9% in 1961, 16% in 1971 and 19% in 1981. Since then there has been a further increase, to 28% of employment in 1996. There is, therefore, no evidence that the increase in the proportion of part-time work has accelerated — it more than doubled in the 1950s and increased sharply again in the 1960s. It should rather be seen in the context of rising overall employment among women — among whom part-time work continues to be concentrated. Importantly, most people who work part-time do so through choice. The June 1996 *Labour Force Survey* quarterly bulletin shows that 71.6% of people working part-time did not want a full-time job, 13.3% were students, and only 13.3% — one in eight — were working part-time because they could not find a full-time job.

A sharp rise in temporary and contract work, another supposed characteristic of insecure Britain, is also hard to find. The OECD, in its July 1996 Employment Outlook, recorded a modest rise in the incidence of temporary employment in Britain, from 5.5% of the employed workforce in 1983 to 6.5% in 1994, but also noted that the proportion of people employed on temporary contracts is lower in Britain than in virtually any other industrial country. In France and Germany, for example, 11% and 10.3% respectively of the workforce were in temporary employment in 1994, in Sweden 13.5%, Australia 23.5% and Spain 33.7%. Temporary employment, in Britain as in other countries, has made a larger contribution to employment growth than previously. There is no evidence, however, that temporary work is becoming endemic. *Labour Force Survey* data suggest a gradual rise in the proportion of people in temporary jobs, to 7.1% in 1996.

Temporary work is becoming more important, but only slowly. There is, in addition, a mistaken tendency to regard all temporary work as insecure. The new concept, favoured by the employment agencies, is to describe temporary workers as 'complementary workers'. According to a report by Corfield Wright, *Flexible Working Means Business*, commissioned by Manpower, the employment agency: 'We see here an opportunity for developing a new type of employment contract suited to a new kind of worker — the permanent complementary worker. The role of employment agencies would be different in this relationship. The agency would employ the complementary worker, providing greater security, more regularity of work and similar benefits to other organisations and would contract with customer companies for their services.' (p.26)

This is already happening to an extent. Many of the 'temporary' workers on the books of Manpower and the other agencies are effectively in long-term employment, with full holiday entitlement and other rights, differing from permanent workers only in that they may not be working at the same location from week to week. In some cases even this is not the case — the agencies operating long-term agreements with companies to provide a constant pool of workers. There is also evidence, in the Corfield Wright report, that complementary workers provide a source of new permanent staff. Rank Xerox, for example, converted 400 complementary workers to permanent staff at a stroke. NatWest Retail Banking Services uses its pool of temporary workers from which to fill vacancies for permanent jobs.

Finally, it was noted earlier that survey evidence has shown that people feel insecure about their jobs, *ergo* there must be insecurity. General opinion polls are, however, likely to reflect back at the pollsters subjects which are being given a lot of coverage in the media. Thus, if job insecurity is a hot topic, people are likely to say that they feel insecure. More detailed survey evidence, however, based on workplace experience, does not support the notion of generalised insecurity. In *British Social Attitudes*, the 13th report, published in 1996, Professor Peter Spencer of Birkbeck College, in a chapter, Reactions to a Flexible Labour Market, analysed a series of responses of specific relevance to the question of insecurity.

On tenure, the results show little change over the 1991-95 period. Among full-time employees, 88% had been with the same employee for a year or more in 1995, compared with 86% in 1991, and rather more, 59% versus 48%, had been with the same employer for five years or more. There was some increase in the proportion of employees expecting to leave their current employer over the next year — 27%, against 25% in 1991 and 23% in 1989, during the boom of the late 1980s. The 1995 proportion was, however, similar to that in the mid-1980s (26% in 1984). In addition, people may expect to leave their current employer for a number of reasons — redundancy is one, but opportunities elsewhere are another. Indeed, of those expecting to leave their current employer, the proportion citing redundancy, 13%, was lower in 1995 than in 1991 (18%) and in the early to mid-1980s (23% in 1983, 20% in 1984, 18% in 1985). Only in 1990, 9%, was the proportion lower over the 1983-95 period. The proportion expecting to leave for a new job, 53% in 1995, was correspondingly higher.

The survey also showed that, in spite of the 'white-collar recession' the professional and managerial classes experience more stable patterns of employment than other groups. Among social classes I and II, 14% of employees had experience of unemployment within the last five years in 1995, similar to the proportion recorded annually from 1983 to 1989, and lower than over the 1990-4 period. For other groups there was also a cyclical effect at work, but from a higher base. Thus 20% of social class III non-manual workers had experienced unemployment within the most recent five years in 1995, compared with a peak of 27% in 1985 and 25% in 1993. For skilled manual workers (21% of whom had experienced recent unemployment in 1995), the results were similar. Job turnover, and periods of unemployment, are much more prevalent, as they always have been, for unskilled manual workers (social classes IV and V, 29% of whom had experienced recent unemployment in

1995, the same as in 1985, but with little indication of any cyclical decline.

Finally, *British Social Attitudes* examined people's attitudes to prospects in their own workplace. In 1995, 23% believed the number of jobs in their establishment would increase, 54% thought they would stay the same, and 22% decline. The 'balance', +1%, compared with 'minus' balances over the 1983-86 and 1990-94 periods, and small positive balances during the boom years 1987-89. The economic cycle, again, is the key to perceptions of job security. According to Spencer, summarising the findings: 'There is little evidence of substantial job insecurity. Despite a high degree of turnover in the labour market, there remains stability of tenure for a considerable group. People now appear to feel more confident about holding onto their jobs — and this improvement seems to have been reflected in a more general recovery in consumer confidence.'

Chapter Four: Problems at the Margin

To deny the existence of generalised job insecurity is not to deny that some insecurity exists, particularly at the margins of the employed workforce. There is evidence that, in recent years, those margins have become wider, particularly for older workers and the unskilled. Older male workers are often specifically targeted in redundancy programmes and find it particularly difficult to break back into work. This was a phenomenon affecting manual workers in the early 1980s (and beyond) and one that has come to be associated with downsizing in financial and other service industries in the 1990s. Banks and insurance companies target the over-50s in redundancy programmes partly because effective occupational pension schemes make it easier to offer early retirement packages and partly because, where downsizing is linked with a change of corporate culture, managers find it useful to dispense with staff who are accustomed to doing things 'the old way'. In one of the major clearing banks fewer than 1% of worldwide staff are males over the age of 50. Nor is this a peculiarly British phenomenon. On OECD figures, the percentage of men aged 55-64 in employment dropped from 70.2% in 1979 to 64.5% in 1994 in Britain. In the United States there was a similar drop, from 70.8% to 62.6%, but in France (67% to 39.1%), Germany (63.2% to 45%), Canada (72.9% to 54.6%), and Italy (just 36.8% in 1979 to 30.7% in 1984), the phenomenon was more pronounced. Only in Japan, 81.5% to 81.2%, did older male workers retain their place in the workforce. Redundancy dressed up as early retirement has been convenient for governments during a period of generally high unemployment, and has often occurred with their collusion. Older workers, a proportion of whom will welcome early retirement, are less of a political problem.

It may be that something of a backlash against this process is occurring, with large corporations, in particular, suffering from the loss of experience that goes with off-loading older workers. Meanwhile, it must be accepted that discrimination against older workers could contribute to a degree of insecurity among all workers — if they come to believe that their working lives are going to be cut short involuntarily.

Just as early retirement has cut participation rates for older workers, so increased staying-on rates and school, and the expansion of higher and further education has had a similar effect for younger people. Even so, unemployment rates remain high for young people. In mid-1996 unemployment among 18-24 year-olds accounted for more than a quarter of total unemployment. On ILO (International Labour Office) definitions, unemployment among 16-19 year-old males stood at 19.9% in winter 1995-96, and 16.1% for 20-24 year-old men. Young people are victims too of the phenomenon of the 'workless household'. Research by Paul Gregg and Jonathan Wadsworth of the London School of Economics shows that, in 1994 18.5% of households were 'workless', often caught in that position by the interaction of the benefits system and only low-paid work being on offer. At the same time, 59.9% of households were 'work-rich', with all adults working, and 21.5% so-called 'mixed-work', with some adults working but one or more not doing so (including what used to be thought of as the 'typical' family with working husband and non-working wife). OECD data show that a third of unemployed young people are in households where no other adult is working.

Finally, there is the position of the unskilled in the workforce. The issue of globalisation, and its effect on workers without qualifications in all the western industrial countries, has been much debated. Nobody disputes that unskilled workers are at a disadvantage suffering, as we have already seen, from greater job instability than other groups. It is not clear, however, that the relative disadvantage of the unskilled has become more pronounced in recent years. Figures quoted by Peter Robinson in the London Business School *Economic Outlook*, November 1996, show that the unemployment rate for males without qualifications doubled to 12.2% in 1979-82, from 6.4% in 1975-78, rising by a half again to 18.2% for the 1983-86 period. The rate dropped to 13.5% in the 1987-90 period, before climbing again to 17.4% for 1991-93, below its peak in the 1980s.

Chapter Five: Britain's Flexible Labour Market?

Insecurity and flexibility, as noted earlier, are wrongly seen as opposite sides of the same coin. If there is no generalised job insecurity, does this also mean that there has also been no increase in flexibility? It does not. While the claims about insecurity have been exaggerated, there is genuine evidence of increased flexibility on the British Labour market.

A series of reforms, of union legislation, social security, employment rights and minimum wage protection all come under the general heading of flexibility. Trade union reforms — the 1980, 1982, 1988 and 1990 Employment Acts and the 1984 Trade Union Act — restricted picketing and the operation of closed shops, reduced union legal immunities and introduced pre-strike ballots. Further legislation is planned to introduce the concept of 'proportionality' into law (if the cost of a strike to the public and other injured parties is disproportionate to the claim and the cost to union members of pursuing it, the union could be forced to pay significant amounts of compensation). Union reforms have gone hand-in-hand, although have not been entirely responsible for, a sharp decline in union membership from its peak of 13.3m in 1979 to around 8m. Social security reforms have included linking benefits to prices rather than to (faster rising) earnings, providing a bigger carrot to take up paid employment, while tougher eligibility criteria have provided the stick. Employment protection, as noted earlier, kicks in after a longer period of continuous work for the same employer compared with the previous position — eligibility for all employment rights requires two years of employment for both full-timers and part-timers, compared with six months and a year respectively in the 1970s. 'Hiring and firing' should have become easier for employers. Finally, wages councils have been abolished in all but the agricultural sector, making the United

Kingdom one of the few countries where there is effectively no minimum wage legislation.

Proponents of the view that Britain's labour market has undergone a fundamental change offer a series of arguments, mostly based around the view that the structural, or non-accelerating inflation rate of unemployment (the NAIRU) has declined in Britain in recent years, both relatively and absolutely. Thus, William Waldegrave, Chief Secretary to the Treasury: 'The evidence is that structural unemployment has been falling in this country while it has risen elsewhere. The nature of the economic evidence means it can never give a completely certain and up-to-date answer. But we can see that the economy has been growing for over four years, but inflation has been kept in check; wage inflation has come down to levels that most commentators thought beyond reach for the British economy; there have been falls in the regional dispersion of unemployment. So the regional labour shortages which were such an issue in the 60s and 70s are much less likely to be a problem. We also see the benefits of the flexible labour market in the big reductions we've seen in the levels of long-term unemployment. Comparing the peak in the early 1990s with the peak of unemployment in the mid-1980s: the number unemployed over one year was down 20%; the number unemployed over two years was down 31%, and the number unemployed over four years was down 43%.' (Speech to Market News service seminar, September 12, 1996).

Labour market flexibility has, according to ministers, been responsible for a multitude of good things. It explains why unemployment fell much sooner in the economic recovery that began in 1992 than in the parallel recovery which started a decade earlier, in 1981. It explains why, so far in the 1990s, the unemployment-earnings trade-off has been so much more favourable than in the 1980s. It explains, as Waldegrave noted, why unemployment in Britain has fallen while in most other European countries it has risen. And it is one of the principle reasons for the attractiveness of Britain as a location for inward investment. Let us take some of these claims in turn.

The British economy returned to growth in the second quarter of 1992 and, against expectations, when it was just below the 3m level, unemployment began to fall in the early months of 1993. By late 1996, the level of unemployment was 1.9m, a drop of over 1m from the most recent peak. By comparison, the recovery of the 1980s began in the second quarter of 1981 with unemployment at just over 2m. Instead of falling as the economy recovered, the total continued rising for more than five years, peaking at 3.3m in mid-1986. The pattern and strength of growth was not noticeably different between the two recoveries but the labour market response was. Why was this so? One explanation has to do with demographic factors — the unemployment problem in the 1980s was exacerbated by a 'bulge' of young people, the baby-boomers of the 1960s, entering the labour force. A second explanation lies with the better use by the government of so-called active labour market policies, including programmes such as Restart, introduced in 1986, targeted at the long-term unemployed. Third, the pattern of downsizing in the 1990s encouraged some workers to drop out of the workforce, including older workers who were retired early.

This leaves, however, a significant role for labour market flexibility. An article in the December 1996 *Labour Market Trends* by Julian Morgan of the National Institute for Economic and Social Research, Labour Market Recoveries in the UK and other OECD Countries, concluded that around a quarter of the improvement in unemployment performance in the 1990s was due to lower participation rates for both younger and older workers, but that the fall was also 'consistent with increased labour market flexibility'.

Another sign of flexibility, according to the government, is the improved trade-off between earnings growth and inflation. In late 1996, when the level of unemployment, as noted above, was just above 2m, the annual rate of earnings growth was 4%. For three years, earnings growth had remained in the 3% to 4% range, even as unemployment was falling. On the previous occasion that unemployment had been just above 2m and falling, in the late 1980s, earnings growth was 9% and rising. Again, there are several possible explanations for this. A key determinant of the level of pay settlements is actual and expected inflation, measured by the retail prices index. The 1990s recovery was characterised by low inflation, and this was expected by wage bargainers to persist, so a lower level of pay settlements, and thus earnings growth, was to be expected. There is also evidence that Britain's two-year period of membership of the Exchange Rate Mechanism (ERM) of the European Monetary System, while generally considered to have been a significant economic policy failure, was responsible for a shift in wage-setting behaviour. The 'new mood of realism' insisted upon by employers faced with the twin pressures of recession and a challenging, and apparently devaluation-proof, exchange rate, was responsible for earnings growth dropping from more than 10% in 1990 to 4% by early 1993. A third explanation is that the fall in unemployment has given a misleading picture of the strength of the labour market. The government's own employer-based data suggests that, during the period when unemployment fell by close to 1m, *employment* rose by little more than half of this, with the increase concentrated in part-time jobs. Employment has been weak, therefore earnings growth has been low. In addition, the regional distribution of unemployment has been more even in the 1990s, with less scope for pockets of overheating (such as the South East in the 1980s) to drive up wages in the economy as a whole.

These factors are worthy of consideration, but they are by no means conclusive. Inflation was low for prolonged periods in the 1980s but earnings growth was never as benign as it has been in the 1990s. Annual earnings growth, in fact, never dropped below 7.5% in the 1980s, even during times when inflation was 3% or below, and the government was apparently as determined to keep it under control as now. Secondly, the ERM explanation provides a reason, apart from recession, why earnings growth fell so sharply during the

1990-93 period. It does not explain, however, why pay did not rise at a much faster rate under the impact of economic recovery and sterling's post-ERM devaluation when, on previous experience, economists would have expected much more rapid growth in earnings. Finally, although there has been a mismatch between the fall in unemployment and the rise in employment, it is not as great as the government's employer-based evidence suggests. The *Labour Force Survey*, generally regarded as a more reliable measure, showed that the first three years of recovery produced a 768,000 rise in employment, not far below the fall in unemployment. As for the improved regional distribution of unemployment, surely that in itself is a symptom of a more efficient labour market?

Earnings behaviour has, then, genuinely shifted. The 'new mood of realism' is real. Indeed, it is perhaps the best single indicator of flexibility in Britain's labour market. According to Morgan again: 'The behaviour of wages is also consistent with an improvement in the functioning of the labour market. Real wage growth has been slower in the 1990s than it was in the previous decade and compares well internationally.' (p.538)

The recovery of the 1990s was the first to bear the fruits of the labour market reforms of the 1980s. The evidence is that these reforms have led to improvements in the flexibility and responsiveness of the labour market. They have not, however, suddenly produced US-style labour market flexibility in Britain.

Chapter Six: The Myth of the 'Anglo-Saxon' Labour Market Model

In the 1970s, the United Kingdom had a rigid, over-regulated and heavily unionised labour market, characterised by industrial disputes and inefficiency, that became symptomatic of the British disease. In the 1990s ministers can claim, as Ian Lang, President of the Board of Trade, did in 1996 that: 'Our degree of labour flexibility is unsurpassed,' and Britain is held up, in some quarters, as a model for the successful reform of a moribund economy whose energies were consumed in internal battles. The British labour market is the least regulated, among major economies, in Europe. Structural unemployment has dropped, on OECD estimates, from 9-10% in the 1980s to between 6% and 8% now. And: 'There is evidence that greater microeconomic flexibility has created more job opportunities and helped UK labour markets to clear more efficiently since the late 1980s. The widening distribution of working hours, low strike activity, ease of hiring and firing, greater decentralisation of fixing pay and work conditions, and wider wage differentials according to skills and regional variations are clear manifestations of greater labour-market flexibility. This on-going process should help to lower aggregate unemployment as the expansion continues.' (*Economic Survey of the UK 1996*, pp. 103-4)

The mistake, given this improved performance, would be to conclude that no more needs to be done. Structural unemployment remains high relative to its level in the 1950s and 1960s, when it was 2% or lower, effectively full employment. It is moving in the right direction, and could even return to such levels, but it is not there yet.

A bigger error comes with the caricature of the 'Anglo-Saxon' labour market model, implying that in the space of two decades, Britain has moved from rigid inefficiency to a red-blooded, aggressively dynamic US-style labour market. Deregulation is an important step towards flexibility but it is far from the whole story. A report by Cranfield University School of Management, *Working Time and Contract Flexibility in the European Union*, examined a range of indicators of flexible working in Britain, Germany, France, Spain and Sweden. Its conclusion was that, while UK employers had more freedom to adopt flexible working practices, including changes in shift patterns and variations in working-time, the differences compared with the other countries were not great. Thus: 'The evidence would indicate that the UK is amongst the leaders in its use of some forms of flexible working practices although, in reality, there are few areas where the UK is the leading country. In general the labour market shares a European wide trend rather than being way out in front or heading in a different direction.' (p.18)

There are other measures which suggest that Britain's labour market is more 'European' than 'American'. Alison Booth and Marco Francesconi of the ESRC Research Centre on Micro-Social Change at the University of Essex, in a study, *Job Tenure: Does History Matter?*, found that, using British Household Panel Survey data, the average number of lifetime jobs held by British men and women is five, only half of that in the United States, and similar to the four held, on average, by German men during their working lives. This may be changing, with newer entrants to the workforce facing a greater number of job changes during their working lives, but it is changing only slowly.

Attitudes among employees continue to exhibit a high degree of inflexibility. The 13th *British Social Attitudes* report, quoted earlier, showed that only 9% of unemployed people were very willing to take an 'unacceptable' job in the mid-1990s, compared with 24% in 1983. While about 50% of people said they were very willing to retrain, if necessary, to find another job — this proportion has not increased over time. Neither has the proportion of people, about a third, willing to move to another area in search of work. Two-thirds said they would not do so. The labour market may have become more flexible, but the individuals operating within it have not.

The differences between the British and American labour markets, indeed, greatly outweigh the similarities. Employment growth in the United States over the period 1983-95 averaged 1.8% a year, compared with 0.6% in Britain. Britain's employment growth was in line with the average for Europe (although slightly better than that for EU members). Even in the newly flexible 1990s, jobs have grown in Britain at only a third of the rate in America.

Geographical mobility of labour, touched on above, is similar in Britain to France and Germany, and well below that of the US. In Britain, housing market rigidities persist, in particular the low percentage of private rented accommodation, large regional house price differences and the difficulty of undertaking long-distance exchanges for council properties. When they interact with the declared unwillingness of individuals to move to different areas in search of work, the effect is to keep mobility low. Had Britain had a recovery in the 1990s which was as regionally unbalanced as the later stages of the 1980s recovery, similar problems would have emerged. They may yet do so.

The biggest difference of all, of course, is the interaction of the benefits system with the labour market. The American system provides initial benefit cover that is comparable with that offered by European welfare states. In the first month of unemployment, the replacement rate (the proportion of the previous wage covered by all benefits) for the average production worker with a non-working wife with two children is 68% in the US, 77% in the UK. For the long-term unemployed, however, benefits tail off rapidly in the US, but remain at a relatively high level in the UK. Illustrative OECD figures, for example, show a replacement rate after 60 months of unemployment of 17% in America, compared with 77% (including housing benefit) in Britain. The prevalence of the workless household, discussed above, shows that sections of the population can still be trapped in unemployment.

This is a matter of political choice. No government, even the reforming Thatcher administrations of the 1980s, has contemplated exposing British citizens to the kind of harsh welfare choices faced by Americans. It may be that this was the right decision, perhaps the only decision, for a civilised society. But it means that talk of an Anglo-Saxon labour market model, encompassing Britain and America, is a misnomer. The current government has refined the benefits system and introduced a range of in-work benefits to ease the passage of the unemployed into work. It has increased some of the financial penalties associated with unemployment. But the British welfare state is still essentially European in character. Kenneth Clarke, the Chancellor of the Exchequer, set out in his Mais Lecture in 1994, his ambition of combining 'European-style' welfare protection with a US-style flexible labour market. The question is whether the two are, or ever can be, compatible.

Conclusions

This paper has demonstrated that the notion of generalised job insecurity, is a will o' the wisp, unsupported by the evidence. It has also shown that while Britain's labour market has undoubtedly gained in flexibility, there is much more to be done, notably in changing attitudes towards career changes and retraining, in improving the geographical mobility of labour and in further refining the interaction of benefits and entry-level jobs.

The idea of generalised insecurity, indeed, and the way it has been exploited by politicians, may have already worked to the detriment of genuinely disadvantaged groups in the labour force. If the problem of insecurity is presented in a way that it becomes seen as affecting everyone, the political will to introduce properly targeted measures aimed at those groups is diminished. If everyone is encouraged to believe they should be feeling insecure, this can have adverse economic effects, on both employee performance and on individuals' willingness to take risks in their economic decisions.

More importantly, the insecurity story is one that, if taken to extremes, will lead to dangerously mistaken decisions. The idea of turning the clock back, in the belief that reintroducing inflexibilities into the labour market would produce a warm glow of security, could not be more wrong. This is a serious risk. The Labour Party is committed to one inflexibility, the minimum wage, and has, while in opposition, attacked most of the government's labour market reforms, even if it does not promise to reverse them. The European context is also important. Britain has broken, ever so slightly, free from the rest of the EU, by insisting that only other member states adopt the social protocol to the Maastricht treaty. But the working-time directive, pushed through under health and safety legislation, shows that even this freedom is a limited one. For Britain to become more European in the operation and structure of her labour market would be a retrograde step. This is the time to build on the enhanced labour market flexibility so far achieved, not to peg it back.

OCCASIONAL PAPERS

16	*Design Decisions: Improving the Public Effectiveness of Public Purchasing* Taylor, Fisher, Sorrell, Stephenson, Rawsthorn, Davis, Jenkins, Turner, Taylor	£10.00
17	*Stakeholder Society vs Enterprise Centre of Europe* Robert Skidelsky, Will Hutton	£10.00
18	*Setting Enterprise Free* Ian Lang	£10.00
19	*Community Values and the Market Economy* John Kay	£10.00

OTHER PAPERS

| | *Local Government and the Social Market*
George Jones | £3.00 |
| | *Full Employment without Inflation*
James Meade | £6.00 |

MEMORANDA

1	*Provider Choice: 'Opting In' through the Private Finance Initiative* Michael Fallon	£5.00
2	*The Importance of Resource Accounting* Evan Davis	£3.50
3	*Why there is no time to teach: What is wrong with the National Curriculum 10 Level Scale* John Marks	£5.00
4	*All free health care must be effective* Brendan Devlin, Gwyn Bevan	£5.00
5	*Recruiting to the Little Platoons* William Waldegrave	£5.00
6	*Labour and the Public Services* John Willman	£8.00
7	*Organising Cost Effective Access to Justice* Gwyn Bevan, Tony Holland and Michael Partington	£5.00
8	*A Memo to Modernisers* Ron Beadle, Andrew Cooper, Evan Davis, Alex de Mont Stephen Pollard, David Sainsbury, John Willman	£8.00
9	*Conservatives in Opposition: Republicans in the US* Daniel Finkelstein	£5.00